My name is Jamie.
I will be in a play.
The play is about a lion and a mouse.

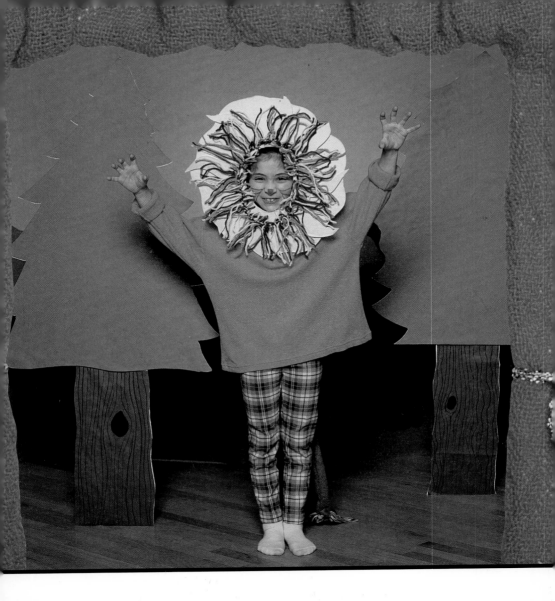

am the brave lion.
am tame.
have a very big mane.

I see the face of a gray mouse.
I see the tail of the mouse, too.
I yell, "The mouse scares me!"

run this way.
The mouse races the same way.
Why does he chase me?

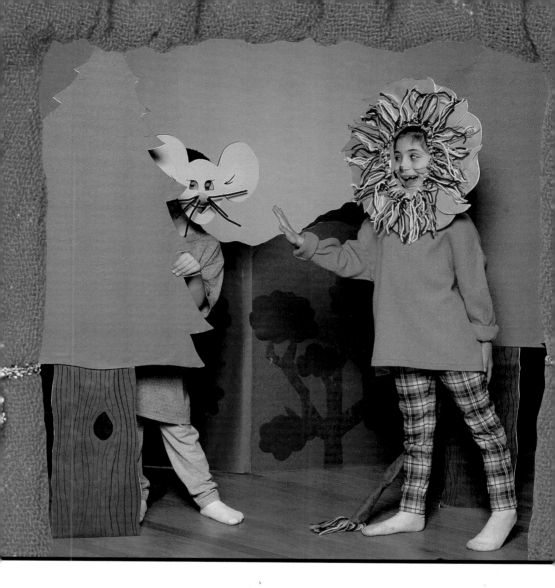

We race and race across the stage.
I wish the mouse would stay away.
This is not a game.

The mouse steps on my tail.
 shake my mane.
 am a brave lion.

The gray mouse takes off his mask.
He shows his face.
The mouse is my pal Jay!

The play is over.
Jay takes my hand.
We will bow and wave.